POSSIBLE SIBYLS

Books by Madeline DeFrees

Poetry

The Light Station on Tillamook Rock 1991
Imaginary Ancestors 1990
Magpie on the Gallows 1982
Imaginary Ancestors (chapbook) 1978
When Sky Lets Go 1978
From the Darkroom 1964

Prose

Later Thoughts from the Springs of Silence 1962
Springs of Silence 1953

POSSIBLE SIBYLS

NEW POEMS BY
Madeline DeFrees

Lynx House Press
Amherst, Massachusetts

Acknowledgements

Some of the poems in this volume were written during periods of support from the John Simon Guggenheim Foundation and the National Endowment for the Arts, to which agencies the author is most grateful. Thanks are due also to the editors of the following publications in which some of the poems first appeared: *American Poetry Review*, *Crabcreek Review*, *Crosscurrents*, *CutBank*, *Graham House Review*, *Hubbub*, *Indiana Review*, *Massachusetts Review*, *Memphis Review*, *New England Review & Breadloaf Quarterly*, *New Letters*, *Northwest Review*, *Pacific Review*, *Ploughshares*, *Poetry Northwest*, *Poetry Society of American Newsletter*, *Seattle Review*, *Southern Poetry Review*, *Sweet Reason*, and *Willow Springs*.

"The Dovecote: Its Head Keepers" first appeared in *Poetry*, copyright 1983 by the Modern Poetry Association.

Library of Congress Cataloging-in-Publication Data

DeFrees, Madeline.
    Possible Sibyls : new poems / by Madeline DeFrees.
    p. cm.
    ISBN 0-89924-079-8 : $16.95. — ISBN 0-89924-080-1 (pbk.) : $8.50
    I. title.
PS3554.E4P67   1991
811'.54—dc20   91-26472
                                      CIP

Lynx House Press books are distributed by:

Bookslinger, 2402 University Ave. , Ste 507., St. Paul, MN 55114
Small Press Distribution, 1814 San Pablo, Berkeley, CA 94702

Lynx House Press, Box 640, Amherst, Massachusetts 01004

For my University of Massachusetts colleagues,
especially Jim, Don, George, Tamas, Andy, Jay and Paul.

Table of Contents

3. Five against the Leash

"Her fond yellow hornlight wound to the west, her wild
    hollow hoarlight hung to the height
Waste..."
                — Gerard Manley Hopkins, "Spelt from Sibyl's Leaves"

"Among [the untrained and uninstitutionalized 'amateur oracles']
were those few...weird and wonderful women known as Sibyls...
They lived in solitude, sometimes in reverenced mountain shrines
that were built for them, or in tufaceous subterranean caverns near
the groan of the ocean, as did the Cumean Sibyl...

"Like oracles, the Sibyls were asked to make decisions on matters
high and low up to the third century A.D. So gristled with moral
fervor were their replies that even the early Christian Fathers and
Hellenistic Jews bowed to them as prophets on a level with those
of the Old Testament. The early Christian church, in particular,
used their prophecies (often forged) to buttress its own divine
authenticity. Even a thousand years later, at the Vatican, four of
the Sibyls were painted into prominent niches on the ceiling of the
Sistine Chapel by Michaelangelo. And...centuries later, copies of
these muscular ladies with their oracular books open used to look
down on the wondering present writer in a Unitarian Sunday
school in New England. Such is the thirst of our institutions after
authorization."
                — Julian Jaynes in *The Origin of Consciousness in the
                Breakdown of the Bicameral Mind*

1. Unpinning the Veil

Whale Watch

The grill of the truck swims into the rearview
mirror at precisely seven
knots and the baleen-breath of the humpback,
an overheated engine, comes on. I try
not to look at the driver: two black lenses,
the blowhole under the baseball cap
where a plume of smoke
rises, and a wrack of kelpy hair. Inside me
something lurches with the weak
cylinder that is bound to break down soon.
Then I'm back to the old
St. Mary's Chapel, trolley wires crossed over
the Gothic window where the world rides downhill
to the city.

       Under the hurricane eye, Leviathan
reminds us, in the world ocean,
all waters are one, no matter what submarine,
minesweeper and territory
proclaim to the contrary. At the sea anemone's
mouth, where the stalk
flares to a trumpet, the hollow tentacles
wave their brilliant locks,
pretending to be flowers. Medusa heads, all part
of a lively diversion, the deadly
feeding apparatus already closing
for the kill.

       Stay down! to the mammoth shape
each of us carries in the salty
blood. *Stay down,* adjusting the clutch, arranging
the sideview. I remember the shadow
passed between me and my prayer, the static
transformed into power. Polarities

of my childhood town,
the dangerous currents charging. Wingspan
of plane or hawk overhead
as I walked to school, dash of the unlucky
heart for its foxhole. I try to believe
that whales are friendly, knowing them bigger than
boat or body, knowing I must
outwit them.

       Riddle me, riddle me, ree: bird
in a bold tuxedo, flightless as a sea-
borne emperor or king. His shy bravado makes
an awkward pet. With him I wore
the black-and-white and on my high Antarctic shelf,
among the generations breeding, dying, slept
encased in ice. Warmer now, these odd eleven years,
I watch the ice-floe drifting to the dark continent
under my body's weight. The killer whale
torpedoes to his target, and I wake again
to the underlying chill.

       I am trying to learn
by subtraction how barnacles cling to a host.
In transparent water, coral
secretes the small skeletons to build a reef. This
monumental work does not work here. The tropical
mangrove, tree that walks all day to the sea
on stilts, does not frequent this shore. The shark
may not initiate attacks on humans, the barracuda
flashing in pursuit is only a fancier pike.
Every turn of the wheel, the light
reveals another zone. The sea,
where life began, is recognized as woman,
is ruthless, and we love her
at our peril.

In the Locker Room

                      I surprise the women
dressed in their bodies: in breasts,
knees, eyebrows, pubic
hair. Excitable children appear
to accept them. Pitted and fat, dazzling
and golden, the women
drowse under the shower, a preview of
bodies the children try on
with their eyes.

            At 65, I am less than
a child, whose mother walked
fearfully clothed, afraid of the water.
My grip on the towel gives me away. I move
into the pool suitably over my head
past my mother's responsible
daughter. Later, wild to learn, I practice
standing alone—only my underpants on—
under the gun
of the hair dryer.

            A queen-sized woman
sweetly accosts me, recommends
more clothes. Someone has pointed out
a peekaboo crack in the men's
locker room. "What a shame," she intones,
"such a nice clean
club." I loiter in my underwear
worn out with surveillance.
What we don't know
won't hurt us.

            Oh, but it does deprive us!
These ravenous mermaids

stripped to their scales, swim from
the framed reproductions, pale and diaphanous
planes engineered for unmistakable
languor. Something has changed
in the changing room where we step out of
lingerie meant for the fainting couch
and bring on the body in person.

The Sand-glass

Running against the wind, sand
blowing towards me,
not really a ground mist but close
though the day is a bright
sound in my ear, pulse or voice,
not quite Thetis, but close—command
from the heard obconical god
part of the long ago: bicameral
mind kept going.

                    And I keep going,
feet in my shoes, a stranger's,
knees liquid as those of Iliadic men
who battle all odds
knowing the tides of fortune
bitter. Not into the scowl of cliff,
the torn surf, nor the river
ooze Virginia chose. What I see below
myself abstracted: the glow removed
until sun through the

                              cavernous eye
of the rock, reflected,
fires and catches on water. Through
the constricted neck like Mercury
announcing the world
turned upside down in the needle's
eye: beggar's heaven
all that I have
received, I run towards the lean
woman, I wanted to stay and be,
run till the sands run out.

The Stirrups

Warts discovered me everywhere by natural right,
the ugly sister's curse, no matter how smart,
how clever, a blight on index finger,
sole of the foot and more intimate parts,
the butt of comic effects I hated, even in Chaucer.
They appeared overnight, uninvited, they settled in,
they bled.

        The workhorse under my girlish weight
changed to a thoroughbred. Held by those broad
haunches and fantasy, I could
forget my warts, believe the night rode out to meet me.
What can I ask of night, if not
surcease from sorrow? Then, onto the scene, came
milkweed, the natural balm, and I was doomed
no longer.

        Every cure I had tried—cautery, knife,
foul-smelling Eskar Ointment, obscure
graves dug for knotted string: milkweed
replaced them all, the miracle-wing of prodigal seed
flung over alley and field.
What flowed in those wild veins, meeting my skin,
restored the clear morning. Heart so full, how

could I guess where the bridle paths led, how far
from the childhood field the horse
returned to a nag? Milkweed grew as before, a universal
weed, the cure no more than a lull
from stubborn warts in my head. Weekly now, my feet
in the stirrups, I lie in the sterile room,
tied to an old specific surrounded by Latin names.

Virus, they say, and *verruca, excrescences of the skin.*

Lie down, they say, and we'll treat you
with strong Podophyllin. Far from the bitter resin,
the poison root, dense properties of mandrake
and may apple, the passion-encumbered fruit. The sense
of the past cut off, this frayed rope in hand,
I grieve

       the live horse released from the dreaming
field to wander the fenced-in waste: the ghost
of something that mattered.

In the middle of Priest Lake

                              Sister Margaret Clare
ships the oars and takes off her veil,
her coif. Not long ago I was her high school student.
Her starched bandeau comes off, wind
riffles her hair. She runs her fingers through
a modified crew cut while I hesitate, eyes
half-closed, unwilling

                    to stare or look away.
"Take yours off," she says. "It feels great!" and
before I know it, I've unpinned the veil, loosened
the coif-strings, lifted the white band
for a sail. I salute the black and white headdress
blown from the mast
of my upraised arm, the freedom

                         I love unfurled
without warning. I'm a lifer committed to sunshine,
to ambient air
as suddenly knowing incurable need
I savor the small pleasure
given up—now given back—in the middle of this lake
miles from the difficult shore
Mother Superior holds fast.

Beside Mill River

When my key sticks in the neighbor's
lock and I finally click, it's the wrong
keyhole, the wrong garage; when my feet,
on automatic pilot,
pause at the common door like the Levittown
ghost who forgets to count, anonymous tenant in a Queens
row house, I conjure up
the unique interior.

When the six o'clock news
overflows every lintel, and the identical chicken
stews in dozens of seasoned pots;
when the Sunday beef
simmers through a slow, canned sermon
I trundle my laundry to the ten-cent Center
or turn again to the run of the river
that is not at all, or almost
never the same.

Except that the river
repeats the memorable
falls over and over—the same cold invitation of moss
and ice. Across the bridge
light flickers darkly
through curtained glass, and I feel the foreshortened
breath drawing me over the edge: the imagined
embrace in the drowned
highrise of sleep.

The Convent at Mystras

Halfway up the mountain—*ingeniously chosen*—or down,
depending how you've come, you find the monastery
where, the guidebook says, we feel *a human presence,*
close. Too close, I say. The whitewashed
walls of cells expected to impress
remind me of the past, mean something else
to me, and I am lost
before the Greek—maybe a monk—who must have
guessed my history and drives me back—west,
the way I'd come.

          I knew I didn't belong in the old
museum to the left, but he was a shepherd:
no straying from the fold. In the darkened nave
a tongue not mine rolled over me, all eyes on the ceiling.
I remembered yesterday's stone wall
rubbed smooth by flocks of lanolin and wool. Steps
in Spain, the stone worn down by sinners' knees.
Of course I fled: through cobbled porticoes, weed,
brambles, rock, to a dead-end
precipice. So much for shortcuts: *this*
inaccessible hill.

          Above the cross, moon stood and sun,
still wearing human faces. I wanted to see
the gift-shop nun, *the faithful guardian*
behind the watered flowerpots
and tourist prose. *Yes, you may take*
my picture. She draws a veil across her chin,
blows out the candle someone struck
like a birthday wish, and goes
to unlock the door.

          I choose a cross-stitched

runner. Rows of stylized urns match the frescoes,
as if the scenes nuns contemplate
had stained their irises eternal. I feel my eyes
glaze over, the nun's mouth
masked like a bandit's. *Twenty-one hundred drachmas.*
In harsh light, I can't avoid the dry
scales under her eyes. No time now for barter. No
quarter in *the Pompeii of Byzantium* for those
who come to ruin seeking a human presence.

Pearl Rushes

1

La peregrina, the wanderer: a pearl of great
price—$37,000—comes beautifully to life
between the breasts of Elizabeth Taylor
where Richard Burton's guests so freely admire
the necklace designed by Cartier. Discovered by
a slave off Panama, the inch-long gem
brought him freedom, but not to

Bloody Mary Tudor, whose queenly hands it passed
through. Naturals are pearl all the way to
the irritant—a bit of shell,
a snail, not sand—but true accidents of nature.
Cultured pearls, on the other hand, are mainly
shell-bead nuclei & a thin veneer
of nacre. X-rays undo the pale skin.

2

Cemented to the shell, the implant can't contrive
a full sphere: it's checked like Australian
aborigines feeding on north coast oysters, who
cracked their teeth, picked out each gem, passed it
to the children for a marble game. Unlike them
the ancients valued pearls over diamonds
& Cleopatra's wealth sponsored the most expensive

dinner party ever. Seated before an empty plate
she removed one earring, crushed it into
her wine, & drank Marc Antony's health. Antony
declined to match Cleopatra's toast
when she turned the opposite ear. Remembering
Rome at the height of pearl fever

diminishes our own. The counterculture

dotes on one earring, but the Romans got there
first. General Vitellius
financed his campaign on his mother's left
earring, worth nearly two
million ounces of fine silver, according to Pliny
the Elder, who cites the ancient
rationale for the pearl's beginning: rainfall

on the open shell excites the oyster to cover
the water-bead—water the heart of the jewel.
Of pearls, Seneca said: "The lobes of our ladies
have attained the capacity to support
a great number." Greedy for kingly gain, rulers
opposed the fashion. In river & ocean
in caged oyster beds, cultivated pearls close on

their seeds. Fear of piracy grows. Japanese
pearls overflow Hong Kong. Trash pearls
with thin coats dyed in mercurochrome
mock the pearl surgeon's blade. From the reel of
high school collections, come others
that never fade—Pearl Noonan, "Teardrop Pearl"
whose haunting contralto floats back

again & again. The plaintive bars of her song
sway overhead in St. Mary's auditorium
where we sat in the grim
folding chairs & waited for breakdown: Pearl
swept offstage in tears while we clapped
& clapped for an encore. Across the salt body
of years, Pearl, yours is the gift I remember—so

pure a jewel it flourished only in private. Take
note, impresarios. In the flip of a coin
success trades places with failure

as Kokichi Mikimoto knew. This son of a noodle
vendor grew 12 million oysters,
enclosing three-fourths of the world's pearls.
Faced with financial disaster,

which was not his oyster, he & his wife stuffed
oysters with foreign bodies
but couldn't explain finding at last their first
spheres. And yet we keep on looking for pearls
in a hail-storm, unaware of the parasite
worm that started good fortune. We hope for
the best in Ceylon, the Bay of Bengal

& the Persian Gulf if we fancy a dive among oil
tankers & minesweepers. The seven-seat
Piper touches down in transparent waters: a
clean aquamarine lagoon in a thin
circle of coral, surrounded by the purple-blue
South Pacific. Véronique, a vice-
president of Van Cleef & Arpels, searches

the island to please special clients, who adore
Polynesia's black pearls: their
depth, luster & orient. "I still buy big
white ones at the Burmese auction." Six hours
later the Piper slides into Marutea
atoll, one thousand miles southeast of
Tahiti. Véronique's countryman,

Jean-Claude, rehearses the usual topics: black
pearls & women. "Women are *mad*
for them," licking his lips on a feast of spiny
lobster & delicate fish
from the reef. In the public area, a guest
eyes the hermits, lifts up his sandalled
feet. Vandal crabs scuttle the floor.

3

"There is no doubt," writes a scientist, "pearls
result from pathological premises. Yet
experts quarrel over the exciting bodies." Liz
Taylor's, perhaps, playing Cleopatra?
But not the healthy ones: "I owe my fine health
& long life to the two pearls
I swallowed every morning," said Mikimoto

dead three decades ago at 96. White, pink &
black, pearls are aphrodisiac
as the friend of a friend who depended on them
discovered in unstocked American
drug stores. From Japan he sent back a sample
ground fine, wrapped in tissue. To mix
long life & sex with danger

clarifies the real issue: the swan-dive of
terrified women in goggles & turbans
who calmly hurl themselves from the rocks, from
Japanese boats. Cutting
their own lives short, they are
survived by the shark-charmers' incantations
moments before the plunge.

After the Winter Solstice

The year unhinged, I wait for lengthening light
under a cloud cover that never lifts
all day—*never* meaning *now* in the darkening
register of night which speaks
for itself.

   Here, speaking for itself, the large
goose in my window
honks and preens. Each side, our gaze cuts through
domestic glass. A female
I think from the tamed bland stare to the white
flirt of her tail. The swoop of crows
could excite us. I am relieved to know this
ruckus is not just chickens. But why me? By whose
runaway logic are we prepared
for this looking-glass trade
of perceptions?

   We stood squared off for a long time,
the river behind her,
before I swerved to a white page of webbed feet,
tilt of a body that said
this one can plunge and she did.

Swimming in Categories

The trust these women float past in could break
your heart, your banker. *Leave your*
cloth's in a locker, management warns. I invest
25 cents, moved by the woman who can't find
her Birkenstocks. I promise her mine
molding in a closet at home,
climb into the pool for Water Exercise, open to
everyone. Today we've drawn
one man and 23 women, mixed bags for the shallow
water calisthenics. After a long
stretch—45 minutes—I find that I can't find my
pulse. This could be serious.

                              I stagger to
my favorite second lane, vacant, swim my Senior
sidestroke until a bald
citizen, lean as a Lifesaver, flashes a turbulent
crawl, spouting whale-like all over
the pool, and sends me
gasping to the gutter nearly drowned in his
wake. Liability without glasses, I see
it's time to move over, clearly admit my mistake.
Beware the macho hotshots: VERY FAST.
Hugging the near wall,
I glide another length, flip to

                                   my elementary
back, beyond the last rafter, the blue-and-gold
pennants waving to safety. Struck
by the wild appendages of another
vaulting dome, I bail out, heading west towards
open space where the woman
with big breasts, who wears glasses, black suit,
and a shower cap for aerobics,

stands up to her shoulders in water for those
who are not serious. I won't make the team, but I'm
not here to socialize. Noting
her firm skin, I could swear

                                she's under 65. I
want to ask her, "Are you an
Adult?" but hesitate, afraid she may have a pin
in her hip, insult added to injury.
Knowing the next step could be critical, I follow
the longer of two bold signs into
a shower room. Thank God for a pretty woman with
twisted foot weaving the maypole spray!
Near the wall, leg braces wait the return of
dependents. I decide to call it a day, come back
when it's straight Seniors & Disabled,
not Seniors, Disabled, & Adults.

Monasticism in the Western World

To support the contemplative life, the Order of
St. Clare in Corpus Christi, Texas,
mixes pleasure & business, breeds miniature

horses. They come in all horse colors & two
varieties: a sturdy draft type & a fine-boned
more elegant strain—the smaller, the more

expensive, no taller than a Great Dane. A high-
priced stud named Red Man Jr. sees eye to
eye with a goose, though not on religious matters.

You can't housebreak them. On page three-eighty-
six of *National Geographic*, Little Hot Stuff
checks into a cage at the desk of Eastern

Airlines. Sandalled & veiled, the vicaress
waits—a cord at her waist—for the claim ticket.
They are flying to a show. Imagine the pair

over Hells Canyon, serenely meditating, at home
in the air, munching on oats. In the next
photo (right) Little Hot Shot, who is

not Hot *Stuff*, nuzzles a rocking-horse muzzled
on wheels. Little horses are very big
deals—$3,500 for a regular mini. Meanwhile,

back at the monastery, horses in stalls, not
wholly ascetic, whinny at landscapes
painted on walls. They are learning to

levitate. The minor thirds of Gregorian chant
hum in their spirited bones. The Order converted

a sad 20 acres, helped by a loan, built a stable,

started with a single stallion & 15 mares. Now
they sell as many as ten minis a year.
Little Hot Shot's sire brought 30 thousand;

Shot, a mere seventeen-five. Whether you want
a pet or a mascot, why not join the parade
to the monastery? You can depend on these

faithful companions, so easy to control, so
willing, pulling the sulkies past
the grandstand. Anyone at all can handle them.

Spiritual Exercises

Knees up! Sophie shouts. We're jogging in place,
one mild gigolo and a pool full of women—
teens to seniors—with every physique
in the book. Madison Avenue gods call our drill-
sergeant a Full Figure. I call her
No Jiggles, read *solid state.* Strong as a
tugboat with plenty of
cargo in tow, she's pulling us through
holy routines: Little-Engines- clenching weak
ankles -That-Could- tie themselves in
French knots.

        Flat on the bottom! Sophia yells at
our feet, her short blond cut
unruffled as the blue cool of ecstatic eyes.
Is it *my* bottom or the pool's? I can't
see through the roily water past the hard rock
drowning out measured
instruction. Just when I'm sneaking a look at the
hour, she tells us to do
Pendulums. Elbows flexed, lifted high, my lower arms
sweep inward and out: Grandmother Clock in
brassy precision.

        Tanned statuesque, the Amazon
goddess floats her breasts on water
I try not to swallow. Birds flutter from nests of
Mother Wren's arthritic fingers. When music turns
mellow I know that we're cooling down to
the moment for gliding: *left, swoop, pointed toes,*
wrists leading the body to
paradise-under-the-shower. *Ole!* I say, meaning
Oil-of-, fighting the locker room bull,
lathering supple attachments. A long stretch for the
beach towel, heavenly clothes.

The Way to the Parking Lot

leads past the sibyl of the tennis court.
They have managed to put her away with
the press and the racquet. Even so, her
double-edged breath
curls the remarkable air, and we know
who is burning the issues is more than
a crazy old woman.

                The tennis court sibyl
is tired of keeping score, of backhand
strokes, intermediate doubles. Believes
the small truth in the loudest
voice to an oracle
lies in the system for amplification.
She wants a clean-air
act to protect her interests.

                      That takes
matching money. She thinks of teaming up
with the sibyl of the cage,
a regular geyser, the same whose claws
were lately removed by court
order, the day they de-fanged her. She
sits on her three-legged
stool spinning woolly

                    strands into a yarn
the gods are pleased to defend
when color persuades, knitting the dyed
balls into garments the world
puts on like air her breath engages. This
morning all over the lot
as in days gone by, she hangs in there
a cloudy medium.

Poet-in-Transit Heading for Zero

The equations of motion that govern a cooling
cup of coffee must reflect the system's
destiny....Temperature must head for the tem-
perature of the room, and velocity must head
for zero.—James Gleick in *Chaos: Making a New*
Science.

You sketched the London scene over the airport
phone last week when you spoke of
the velocity of our lives, meaning yours
and your lover's. You'd written
a Christmas memoir for *Seventeen,* climbed
mountains in Alaska, looked into a crevasse.
You'd be in *Vogue* again.

                          The hospital stay
brought us up to now—transcontinental flash.
Your voice from the glass booth
rang hollow, bounces still off walls of my
skull—enclosure so vast no hat would fit
as the milliners of my childhood
can testify. By contrast

                          my life looks tame,
has the pick-up & tempo of its own
broken routines: the clean
blue flame of the Natural
Gas Company sign, steadily revolving: all the
glitter hemmed in like radioactive pellets.
I'm not jealous—only rueful
now & then, having made my bed and lying in it.

We considered the scar on your breast—purely
precautionary—that interfered with your

pleasure in the womanly gifts you were given.
Trust surfaced between us, that long-distance
heaven we're headed for over mountain & crevasse.
I was leaning hard into every
word—and grateful.

Dear friend, when the moving
picture you are in turns frenetic, remember
the straits back home and the rain
you are loyal to. When the whole world
steps on the gas, and the pace of my attenuated
life goes beyond my power to
handle it, I look east to your light, the line
of my unlisted number open for your call.

Living by the Water

The reservoir we drank from fills
and fills again, unending
as the coastal rain that swells it.
The water-table rises, old roads washed out
and small craft swept to sea.
Until the storm front passes, let me stay
clear of your tilted deck: no other way to be
left out of the one place I cannot
walk on water.

                When we slept, dry-eyed
on the shores of Babylon, how did we
hang our harps on the willow branch in this
strange land? Pale reed
beside the water, my water-sign
a wand depending on the hidden spring.
I see how water carves the wale
of the corduroy cliff and throws
great boulders on its wheel

                      to round
these urns for burial. How water lifts
columns of basalt, cutting its own
bright path, jagged down the mountain.
My fingers graze the smooth amphoras in these
tidepools, Greek to me. I feel the darkness
coming on. Like the sea,
I gather wool and the wool I gather is another
kind of crying to that gull

                    sailing the lower
air and dying slowly back into the wave.
I blame these phases on the moon but can't deny
the tides we've known. A circle in her beak

brings water, sharp horns
mean wind. This is the place we started out,
the place we've always been. And now good-bye,
the path forks here. I am my own
barometer, and like the water, always falling.

2. The Body's Weather

In the Whirlpool

Focused on the middle distance, my eyes avoid
her airspace. My toes collide
with another human
foot. Quickly, I withdraw the look
lost between clock and infinity. "Sorry,
I wasn't paying...Do you
swim every day?" Her name is Eva Perl.
Her accent is German. Now that we're warming up
I brag—modestly—"I started at nine
laps and have just leveled off
at thirteen."

           Her gaze is straight on. "I have
no ambitions," she says,
the sheen of her hair floating
silver in steam. It is not a rebuke. She may
be a sibyl. "I'm 78 and lucky
to swim at all." Silence returns
the machine we are part of, caught in this
distance, the bubble and fall,
an ocean between us. I want to bridge it.
To follow this Eva

           preparing to leave. "I hope
I'm like you when I'm 78."
She looks back without smiling. "It's been
by ups and downs," she remarks climbing up.
I think of the photographs—the heaped
anonymous fingers and feet. Of what is required
to move past intrusion. The mother-of-pearl
luminous coat, shell that encloses,
the wall I must build
to come to terms with this alien body.

The Widows of Mykonos

Seeing their black weeds in terrible sun, the other
life that holds their gaze
unswerving in the village street, I recognize
the miles I've come to find this land
Henry Miller calls *all stone*
and light.

            My steps are sagging stone, meandering
through the patterned square, my heart
not light but shrouded, a house closed up, its flutter
caught in that familiar net
of shuttered grief.

                  The skyborne song turns hollow
in a maze of stone, the light a torture
and the dark a cave. I carve the epitaph in some
illusionary code
the scholars cannot break and bury what remains
under toppled stone.

                  Legend in stone relief, light
breaks in half across the blue Aegean,
night floods the whitening shore. Along stone walls
the full-face light, without slant or shadow,
falls, leaving no stone unturned.

Hagios Panaghiotes: the Church in Tolon

Feeling nervous, out of place and halfway through
the Greek orthodox Sunday service, I realize
from certain headlong illuminations
I'm on the wrong side—the men's—but not enough
to do anything
important. At the votive stand, a widow
blows out candles, lights a few, the order
random as the genuflections of the priest, and I
am in a foreign land.

                    Ensconced in a separate
altitude, the cleric gives us
his back, small acolyte on the line, bobbing
when the leader
bobs. Through his beard, the priest intones
familiar versicles. As in a Breughel
painting, what matters
happens on the edge. The cantors
cant. The women move their lips in silent
intercession. The shady incense drifts
above our heads.

                  Demented chandeliers: crystal
and gold in clouds of plastic. The bearded
saints look down—martyr and mystic—bald, severely
drawn. All of us are old. The operation
was successful, but the patient
stars flicker to a halo in the dome. Long ago,
schooled to fight distraction
to levitate—that is, *make light*, as in Marvell's
Center of Knowledge—I learned to wait
on the dead. Light the candle one more time.

Knitting the Sleeve of Care

Swept to the surface by too much light, I wake
with my head in my hands. Cars across the river
veer through the green
night. Creak of the floor over my bed, beside it
the patient shuffle of digits, and overhead, the four
feet of the stroke victim's
aluminum cane.

                The hounds' long leap
streaks past my window under No Trespassing signs
where the current calls the other way, and the red
glare of sumac flags a jogger upstream. Better to go down
gasping for air, your whole life flashing before you
than fall under the wheel of the trucker
making up time as he goes.

                    I am making up ours
from channels under my eyelids, insomniac
drives, the moonlanes of traffic
rising up in the vertical night. Now the highway
unravels and lets down the ropes of a swing
depending, fragile as thread, from scissoring
branches I see through

                  as the bulk of my body
travels the track of a comet
released from unbearable height. These faraway
rumors, these emanations: are they
fear or vertigo? Such animal grace
dissolves along the borders towards the deep
ending we dream at the close of every day.

A Visitor's Guide to the Lewisburg Cemetery

Not a sparrow falls...and my heart takes off
into another country. The heaven or nothing
writes a vapor trail over the river
vault. The riddle Shelley hoped to crack
that time with Jane Williams
when he talked of tipping the boat—"Now
let us solve together the great
mystery!"—and Jane got out to wade ashore.
The cryptic figures chiselled on stone
by the body's weather. Your number is up,
the saying goes, and the dice, like the gun
in Russian roulette, already loaded.

Finding my way through the graves to the
church and not the reverse, I come
to the granite slab marked FEINOUR. And Yes,
I say, it's as good as any, a faint
wind skewing black oaks on the hill
overlooking the steeple. Moss and tendril
already creeping into my legend: November 18,
19—19—repeating digits, a tic
in the temple. In the space of a hyphen
characters soften, the tool in my hand,
a power drill running away with the motor,
carving the fatal numbers.

In this leaptide the paired 8's balance on
their torsos, and needle-thin,
the obelisks raise acronyms above the crowd.
Amid a clutch of verticals, I call
that horizontal man the Sleeper of the Year.
His landlord neighbor runs
lead pipe around a plot to keep the vagrant
footsteps out. Cold light breaks through.

When a cardinal whistles
low in my ear and a skylark answers, I know
this is all in the head I am out of
here in the hectic west wind of the graveyard,
wandering out-of-the-body.

From the People's Memorial Association

"Would he fit in?" the English professors asked
checking on a poet friend. What they meant:
Could he last through an afternoon
in the clear dry air of that sectarian campus
without a drink, without a nicotine
fit? "He's...sociable," pretending to miss
their drift. Let them be
more direct.

        Headdress askew, head in the blue
my nun's black veil
turned the wrong colors, what under the sun was
the matter? "*When* will I fit?" I asked, meaning
at last in my coffin? Would the rites include
adjusting the length of my reach, a hold
on my tongue? could anyone teach the meek members
subjection?

        Feast of Saints Peter and Paul, why
do they come to me now—words of the old
priest rehearsed, martyrs on call, there in the
convent chapel: " ...crucified
head downward...unworthy to die like his Master..."
Fitting and proper, I say, but there's
more: "...died by the sword..no small thing...
having your head

        chopped off..." Walking outside
my mind adrift, I try to guess the precise
number of foot-candles
lighting my steps to the grave. Three by six, it is
no small thing. Ashes riding the wave
I find myself choosing fire over earth, sea over
metal, the urn of my ribs too strict,
heart too wide for the grey processional of this
Seattle morning.

Shadegrown Tobacco

For Richard Hugo

Tobacco wraiths are back. Their pale arms
flutter in the gauzy field
and you are in your 14th dream, the letters
white confetti round your bed. I want to say:
Cured, the wide green leaves of this New England
shed, old rituals call us to the place
we started out, the edge.

                         I'm walking in a gale.
The metal STOP signs flap like paper
by the cold motel where I step into the traffic.
The flag reads: HEMLOCK   DEAD END STREET
All the great men of our past—Washington, Monroe,
Jefferson, Taft—cross and re-cross the thoroughfare
on their way to the wild
Pacific where you are. I'm coming too.

                                 The gulls
own Haystack Rock, this coast belongs to me. You own
a run of jacks, their grey mouths
own the sea. No thread-and-scissors men,
these three in oilskins who tend
and spin the giant vacuum, suck dirty air or water
from the storm drains.

                           The severed line may not be
vital but a fatal twist cuts off
the span their laws determine. Not Zeus himself
can overrule the fates, nor madness rescue.
Opponents rise like dragon's teeth in furrows. More
myths you would have said
you didn't know, pretending

not to read.

       Ecola park: tobacco wraiths move west
where great ferns cluster
on the woodland path. I watch them
laying down their swords
and in the aftermath, dark berries of salal.
No one owns the wind you love. The phantom lung
demands its fill of air. Shrill kites
own the clouds, and sheer
sun falls into ocean.

       You would have loved these three
hard-drinking men, nothing phony about them:
a crew you'd like to spend time with
in a bar. And now you've crossed it in your fancy
salmon boat. Or better yet, waded out into the stream
leaving us with the big dreamfish
you and Yeats were after.

       Wherever I am, Dick, I want you
to know I'll keep you close as a coat in grey weather,
your voice strong in my ear, falling
like these coastal rains
to fill the reservoir or float the Big Sky home,
riding your favorite thermals. The clouds,
not gauze or birds of prey, but raw
silk umbrellas gliding the wind, the shroud lines
tough and holding with your abandoned towns.

Blueprints

From a long way off I can see the cross-
hatching. This anonymous man of the Plain
People of Lancaster County laid out

more than 100 barns, not depending on blue-
prints: *It's just a talent the Lord gave me.*
I can close my eyes and see the whole

structure sitting there. Sitting there,
alert for the whole structure, I count
33 question-mark forms under wide-brimmed hats

bent to a common task against the Prussian blue
blank of sky. My fingers trace a slow X
of suspenders, the unknown articles of risk

and faith in a landscape of minor mercies. *This*
one touched my heart, says the planner, asking
that his name be forgotten. The barn

belonged to a burned-out widow. People came from
miles around. The barn was raised again, clean
grain of the wood stood vertical, all knots

wrestled into a pattern. Translating this morning
the visual text into words, I ask that my name be remembered,
that the legend over my grave

be the planner's. *This one touched my heart.*

This Paper White Narcissus

                                    cut from a forced bulb,
placed in the Spode bud vase you brought,
beside the gilt madonna on permanent loan, brings
the room alive with the rumor
of your death—by violence, as it happens.

When we stayed the night in Bigfork, our last real
visit, you took guest towels for the two of us
from a pine box upended. *How do you like my coffin?*
The casual tone, calibrated
for shock, told us we were hand-picked to witness

you, center of another drama, so we joked: *Buy now,*
pay later—something like that—then unpacked
our gifts while you added a pound of butter to your
pound cake. It was April, cold sun
low over the lake entrance to Glacier under shallow

snow cover. Now you are...*the second priest in ten*
years to disappear under mysterious
circumstances. I hear the telephone call
echo in English, your last words to the housekeeper,
then...*Missing in Mexico*, the headline a Butte

release sent clipping across the continent, then back
west, wired, I guess, from Cuernevaca
where you'd spent five years in medical retirement.
I'm real disappointed we didn't find

the body. This, from the bishop, seems clear as
daylight shows the dim porch bulb, lit by a photo-cell
gray light turns on in Seattle. What do you
ask of me here, five months murdered—or possibly
not—no matter what the authorities say.

What have we left to settle? I see you coming back

to contradict the bishop: *if not murdered, certainly
dead, away from his medication.* I re-read the white-
paper myth: *His blood soaked the earth, and up
sprang the white flower with its red corollary...*
If this is the death you willed, stick to your story...

from which an unguent balm is distilled. I'm waiting
for the final curtain, every road repeating 55
Alive, every night waiting, dreaming Flathead Lake
under the Wedgwood lamp you gave me. By the way, I wish
you were here to admire the new shade.

What I Mistook for Heather

was creeping thyme, the gardener said,
and I watched it creeping
over the sheer rock fall without a leg
to stand on. "So delicate," a neighbor
said, preferring thyme to sturdier
plants, the day she made that confident
pronouncement. Just out of sight
the raspberry canes waited for something
to lean on. When I planted my foot
in the flowerbed, it felt like the first
far step across the moon.

Gallery of the Sarcophagi: Heraklion Museum

Worse luck. The first bathtubs I've found in Crete
and both in use by nice clean skeletons,
their knees drawn up, their feet deliberate
as a will. In old museum bulletins
these long-term bathers join a stunned élite
remarkable for simple elegance
beside the ornate bull, the double axe
vendors display in all the tourist racks.

I must confess I find the crowd more numerous
than perceptive. Impossible to spurn
these bones the centuries have bleached so glamorous
that sternum should adorn a Grecian urn.
I'll tap this...*effigy* upon the humerus:
Move over, Ma'am—or Sir—you've had your turn.
Call the museum guard, evict the squatter.
Impound the cameras and bring on the water.

I thought the beehive tombs serenely tidy,
the ossuaries, awesome as a nun.
If only I had roamed the Alps with Heidi
or scaled the Matterhorn, it might be fun
to scramble over rocks from here to Friday,
though twice I've been cremated in the sun.
This trip laid out till dark, an early wake,
is one I can no longer undertake.

I knew a woman once whose husband yearned
to join her in that private act—a shower.
For weeks she would refuse while passion burned
the helpless spouse. What if the house caught fire?
Would neighbors understand the world had turned
the doubly cleanly higher every hour?
Or would the coals of passion sink to shame

scorching the children and the family name?

To exercise the dead we have mislaid
and use our wits to help them make a landing
on eternity, no matter how afraid:
last week I read of corpses trussed and standing
on their heads in jars like so much marmalade.
The method, I suppose, is one worth handing
down—unfit for certain claustrophobics.
The active wait in line to try Contained Aerobics.

Sometimes the body's laid out like a hero
sandwich. At others, neatly wrapped in pit or grotto.
The best-dressed corpses in the west since Nero
prefer to make the journey obbligato,
fall on a word, a sword, the instant zero
ground approaches—or back upon a motto:
Abandon soap, all ye who enter here.
No sheets, no shoes, no service. Try our bier!

Not Agamemnon murdered in the bath
can change my mind about the promised soaking.
Not Achilles, sulking in his wrath,
would dispute the point of honor I'm invoking.
There comes a time along the beaten path
when a woman needs another kind of stroking.
All the world's a tub where Dead Rights play small parts,
and win or lose, it's how I choose to patronize the arts.

The Dovecote: Its Head Keepers

One pulled mad from the Rock in a spiralling storm,
most keepers took six months of the early
watch, or more, then applied for transfer. Not
strict enough in that superior dovecote,
they might ignore men out of pigeon holes or uniform,
might let the sea proceed
without direct surveillance.

                          The dovecote teemed
with gulls. Christened at birth *Marinus A. Stream*,
one keeper served May to December, 1894.
Home for Christmas maybe—anyway, far from the Head
and the 100-sheer-foot drop from offshore
Tillamook Rock where a lowered boom
decided the menu. Where pulleys tied to ships
standing off at a safe distance,
delivered tons of Clackamas stone that might hold out
against those heavy seas.

                          Mostly they counted
days. Jailbirds, they screaked with gulls
riding the crazed beam with the phantom
goose. Took turns cooking bad food, swallowed the same
fear: midnight on the spiral stair
seen like a conch from below. The archivist
writes, "The register of lighthouse
keepers in our custody…" ends in the middle, 1912.

All of them grieved for themselves at the iron
door with the station ghost
where the mill of the surf grinds slowly, and light
outlives the record by 47 years. Except one
Oswald Allik, who kept his head, we must assume,
and stayed two decades. Retired, he made a nightly

pilgrimage ashore to check up on the beacon.

In the boom of the sea, all of the heads are ash, pigeon-
holed in urns, the light gone out in '57. The dovecote
keeps the cold astronomy of loss in place, stars
clustered round the tower. And in the niches there
in homing flight, stars rich enough to pay
25 grand in the grandiose columbarium.

Atlas of Oregon

After a day of horizontal rain
I study the clouds off Cascade Head,
the world's heft on my shoulder.
The ironclad sky armada
drawn from the western edge, crosses
a ridge to the rain shadow. The tide
turning, and wind off the coast
shifting aloft against Olympian odds,
I steady the heavens' weight.

Traveling light: gulls are a fleet
sailing blue through a rift in the slate.
If you think my spine a match
for mountains, bone chained to this body,
this burden, you are right. I am a proud
carrier, not a rocket let go from the silo.
I would lower this globe,
this skull, like air let down, safe
and powder-dry, on the other side.

If the column of bone gives way, the topmost
link broken, may the cloudy beast
return to his stall, graze on the hay
we made while the sun
shone in the middle east and the far
mushroom was a roar, dull as the ocean, rock
still rock, and the Titan's foot
set firm in Pacific waters
where the book of maps begins.

The Leper Graves at Spinalonga

The holy ones, lives written after on the skull
would be off-limits here
where lepers with more money sleep in private
graves. Their skeletons fare worse
than those who lie together: lids pried loose
by marauders from the artificial
caves, wood left to warp in sun. They hawk
the skulls like trophies in the town
across the water until Greek fathers lay down laws
to fence them out.

                The life already written on
my skull, still thatched with hair, at last
uncovered to the sun,
engraves the body deeper every year, the air
ecstatic with the prize
not won. Slowly from this peninsula, the eye
clones a circle to its frame. The algebraic
bones assemble in the well,
the femoral declares itself, and memory
retrieves its thoughtful home.

                   I'd like to play
the prophet in the valley of this death,
call each spine and clavicle
by name: announce, *In spite of all, these bones*
will live again, be covered with
new skin, the slain
come back an army, and from the four winds,
breath. All make-believe I know.
Dry as we are, as good as dead, can anything begin
the slow articulation led by light?

                  The toe

I broke last summer looks shorter knit
together where I climbed the stone in sandals,
a maimed evangelist in Spinalonga
on the run. Back home our leaders lie together,
their plots more private than the leper graves
and not in Arlington. The long disease
continues, fences collapse and walls, no matter
how we guard them. We peddle artifacts
staring from the crater. We are happy
vandals writing history on skulls.

Crossarms

On a cold day, this six-foot stepladder's a hardship
post for washing the bay windows where a rude
bird—probably crow—let fly with droppings
that whitened and blocked the clear
prospect more than a year ago.

Newspapers recycled this morning, I polish the pane
to a fine gloss with rediscovered
poems—carefully chosen pages of APR. The whole sky
reflects in the window: thin wires
cut through the picture plane where a lone crow

watches from the telephone pole's crossarm. This
bird of 23 calls excels in the mimic
arts: whine of dog, squawk of hen, a voice almost
human. Why is he so silent?...Toodle-oo,
Goodbye, Yehuda Amichai, Translated by the Author.

And would you mind, I wonder, my buffing windows with
your lines? After your reading you would not
shake my hand. I felt rebuffed. Religious reasons
says a Jewish friend. Sometimes I do not
understand these tough exclusions.

Your poems make good things happen. The light comes
unobstructed. I couldn't tell you as you
scrawled your name with more I can't decipher on
the first blank page of *Great Tranquillity*. I know
my next step is *Danger: Do Not Stand Here*. I

stand there. *You may lose your balance*. Now *that*
I can understand. Behind me, wind
sways the power lines. The crow holds steady. Ahead,
the poet's face looks out beside "The Water's Surface."

I toss the crumpled papers

at the ladder platform, shift my feet, miss, and see
that noble face go down. My neighbor
passes with a cheery warning. Time to grip the sash,
invoke Negative Capability, inform some other
body: Batman, the Flying Nun, the Wright Brothers.

      Tonight, below the danger line, I'll toss
newspapers into next week's recycle
bin. I check my work with pride. The window gives
everything back. The crow prepares for
flight, wears the committed look of graffiti artists.
Storm clouds move in. Soon the three of us
will sleep as one, our names written on water.

Five against the Leash

On the Freeway, Getting the Big Picture

                    Lightly,
these islands come in from the sea, fumbling
their way through the Sound to
exactitude. They constitute a dependable state
in the knock of rude-running
tides. Which one is the island for me,
spewed up volcanic, loosely
joined to a larger body, the broken colors
fused by the onlooker's eye
to extraordinary

                    light. Driving past Scatter Creek
on my way to the swaying
peninsula, I hear those long-ago islands
dock against the continent. Water
reverberates in dim tunnels
under basalt, channels the path to an opening.
When lava chills on cold
sea water, when thunder
splits against the mountain, the law of opposites
fulfills itself. Pebble conglomerates

                    scramble
with oceanic crust, merge and emerge, thrust
upward in a bold mosaic.
Point by point an islet at a time, the laggard
land is reconciled to water. The bridge
from dot to dot lies in the brain. Though what
my vision recommends may not be
what you see, light bends
the truest colors to a line, a tone: in harmony
these pinhole spectacles

                    accrue on canvas, come
together in a new *Grande Jatte*
to rectify the scatter of the light.

Dialogue Partly Platonic

When we met by chance at the letter
drop on a cold bright
day in early spring, I was in jeans
and a blue beret. I remember your
jacket—suede—when we
walked, surprised by
ourselves on the sudden street, into
each other's arms. Denim and
suede and the time to stop.

In a house more ancient than brick
and beam, where the chant of
cloisters rose and fell
and the stern-browed portraits
looked askance, we circled the crypt
by candle gleam in the intricate
steps of a formal dance, threading
the mazes carefully,
measuring every syllable.

When the record ends and letters fade
when the tape runs out on the poem's
reel where the shadows lie
in the candle glow and the house
embodies its women still, here is
the cave I would have you
know. Re-enter it now, mounting
the steps to your troubled sleep
in the upstairs dark.

Dumb Cane

In this house, nearly a greenhouse, no
paradise although filled with light,
with deliberate plants in their summer,
the wrist-thick cuttings of dumb cane
surround me in pickle jars of sour
water, each with a leaf node utterly
speechless, the green corrosive tendrils
nowhere uncurled but folded as if
in permanent sleep. For the moment
the negative voices hush what the parent
stock has set down as given: We root
in murderous soil, the smell of promised
earth gone bad, growth that chastens
the tongue, endangers touch, refuses
its progeny.

       Between the succulents and
the rubber plant, tending this rent-
free house for a month, the owner far off,
I am struck by the wealth of imperfect
adjustment. By the skill of tools
set aside in the prime of their work,
restored grain of the wood, and beams
that will soon be uncovered. What pardon
stays the razor-edge hammered out
from a trowel? Into what jungle
does this clearing lead when waiting ends
and the quenched devourer sends down roots
into manifold earth? Steward of this
arrested growth, I pinch, poke and water,
nursing the life

       that must supplant me.
Between the sowing and the reaping

I celebrate the mute survival of evil
where twin buds swell, obscene at the base,
their lease on life, attacking the other.
How carefully I propagate the ornamental
killer, chewing the wished-for sweet
towards no words. My gradual tongue
swells, skin revealing the rash
cult of poison when all I need is to say
I love you, go down on my knees
with the scientist persuading the cactus
to give up its thorns.
Like him I believe we are new selves
in a new place.

Convection in a Coffee Cup

When waves shimmer ghost-like above
the radiator of your 1970
Chevy, over sunstruck tar on a summer
shoulder, you monitor fluid motion,
bear witness to the rise
of hot liquid or gas, the phenomenon
known as convection.

                    Your coffee
barely warm on a winter morning, heat
dissipates with no hydro-
dynamic motion. The coffee remains
in a steady state. Should the state be
unstable and chaos ensue
a snake in the mathematical grass

has to be factored into the equation.
Such simple equations as some
scientists knew are really no more
than metaphor. They watched science
stray from the old order
snaking closer to poetry, an order
purely imaginary.

                    This one trusted
his mental pictures. Thus, a snake
head-in-mouth makes a comeback,
rejoining extremes: heaven & earth,
beginning & end, science & art
deep in the heart of numbers. To get
the picture dribble some cream
into this hot cup of coffee.

The Garden of Botanical Delights

1

At the Public Market, salmon in hand, we
examine the *Brassica*,
children of the wild cabbage laid out with
botanical fervor: collards, turnip,
mustard and kale, broccoli, Brussels sprouts
and the queen of them all,
kohl-rabi.

       When I was the bride of Sorrow
and carried his poison
tips in my quiver, the arrows pointed towards
my own unsinkable heart, pain
the proof I needed on the brink of my being
alive with the pulse of
disaster.

       Today in a transparent season,
stalking the stalk plant, I hear
the stream in my veins
run faster. I no longer wish to count
myself a Cabbage Planter—my figure for those
who feel nothing—the too-stolid head
balanced above steady ground.

2

Here is my act of faith in the secret life of
plants, the still more secret
lives we harbor in our sleep when images
float upward into light
and everything that grows
begins to speak: *Tension along the midriff,*

consternation among the broccoli. The several
heads rising from a single
stalk, the many voices of bok choy. We wade
all night into the darkening
window, the living room slowly filled by
the river, cover our bodies

with silt from deepening beds like women who
darken their eyelids with kohl.
The life we hold in common with the common
vegetable tells us to furnish our house
with sun, with air and rain: whatever
the current carries.

3

What is the root of this passion for
classified information, sensors
fine-tuned as hairs on the pods of white
mustard? One scientist
devised a scheme for breaking the genus
in five, alive as the odd-numbered
senses, a plan based on leaf-buds,
on flowers.

      For hours this morning, I
pored over the Lindley charts, a kindly
student of taxonomy. Dearest,
late as it is in love's perennial
summer, all my terminal buds
are active and open, flowers abortive
and succulent, ready
for harvest.

      My vanished lover,
come back to volatile oils
distilled from seeds of black mustard,
to the leaf mustard's
gathered rosette. This cool-season
variety shoots to seed
later than the usual white. Salads
postponed

      you are sorely missed in your
good garden. Like the steady green of a
cover crop, yours was a notable leaving.

4

When the plant dies back into the seed
the missing language flowers. Linked
words stretch their chains across

the continent, the ink and circuitry
of winter culture. Your crisp Italian
consonants roll across my tongue:

brocco, brocco, the shoot that turns
diminutive as broccoli. This singular
crop exists chiefly in the plural,

its Latinate form one of many seeds
from which this poem grows. Hold onto
the root and note the piccolo's

slant rhyme in *broccolo,* the salmon's
uphill climb into receding rivers
and the other name for the wild

ancestor: sea cabbage. Into that tide
I plunge again and again
until the next spring floodtime.

5

If I were one of the herd
turned out by my lord
to pasture, I'd dream of
the drumhead cabbage,
the thousand-headed kale.

Browsing the grassy knoll
I'd find my vegetative
life enough. This
intermittent lack beyond
the livestock in our lives

where far off summits lift
and fall might disappear
as scant light slowly
changed the scale
of what we shall not want.

Then take these flowers,
too long borne like a cross
and hang them where
the brick walls ring
exultant in a dying chant:

I cannot love my yield
the less because of this
late gathering.

Night Work in the Islands

They are carpenter frogs sawing with
miniscule blades on hardwood
and never get through. They are
courting frogs creaking the porch swing
all night long. They are heavy
sleepers, a rasp in each nostril,
breathing in double time
the thin mountain air. They are a
versatile congress of birds
working overtime on the budget.

They are building a chest for the winds
that raddle the palms. They are
launching a lily pad to cradle tadpole
eggs. They are floating delirium
balloons tied to a kite string, to the
crater's rim. Haleakala! *Tch-tch-tch*
A zebra dove interrupts the choir in
the clouds with a chorus of shoulds
like a teacup dropped from a helicopter,
and day breaks again.

The Witness Tree

The tree that straddles Willow Run,
a stream I christened early on,
holds lopped limbs skyward from a base
where root and ledge of stone are one.

The creek divides around the bole,
gathers into a holding pool, and
penetrates the living cell
with mineral calm. Between the roots
the stream moves on, unloading there

its grainy freight. Water assumes
a winter glaze, opaque as sleep
until the sun obliquely joining
Willow Run, scallops the edges

delft and thin, fuses their glow with
porcelain. The pulse of water
underground, reverberates against
the stone. That music snags my
passing glance to crystallized

recalcitrance. Against the rail, I
take my stand, my arms transfixed
before the tree's—intruder on a somber
slate—slow traffic of monotonies.

And whether tree or woman stand, or
both or neither, water knows,
spelling the kingdoms much the same,
no matter how the fences rise.
Should you demand beyond the bend

a stone-cold prospect or a green,

the witness cannot reconcile arrested
waters, fast between the rocky
loam and root grown rock. The stream

must speak its quick reminder from a
sullen bed. Consult that seer
where the water flows.

Like the Astronomer's Tame Elk, It May Be the Only Thing Missing

The oscillation at the threshold of recall
when light begins the little torture-dance
makes all the circuits flash
their urgent calibrations. The archive keeper
mounts the branching stair with taxidermal
patience, no one to hear
the ritual incantation. How the hair
carries the head beyond itself, the applefall
a scent embedded at the root of trees
we can't remember, through the flower leaves
boughs fruit in cycles, halo us like a rack.
Down pathways of the garbled wood,
dense with parasite and lichen, we flick aside
green curtains as we track the startled
animal through game preserves to artificial
fishponds where a catch reflects
unlikely.

       Unlikelier still: Elk en route from
the old estate—no visitant of ordinary
houses—trumpets up the castle stair to empty
chambers where the party was, drinks
black beer, omits a necessary step on the critical
descent, and breaks a leg. Just so
do interferences along the crooked spine
deliver up their dead.

The Ventriloquist's Dummy

Mind was a double-edged sword. The blade turned
outward was dull. The other
turned against the self, stayed keen: the mind
and the voice on opposite sides.
I was caught between. The name of the show was
Humility.

Body behaved like a dog: it must be
kept down. Soul flung a diffident
thread away from earth, anchored on God, on Heaven.
The thread was a given: it must stay
intact. All those years perfecting my circus act
were sawing a woman in half.

Midway through an
opening, some gremlin of the ear
let in Lily Tomlin *speaking clearly into her*
mouthpiece. I was tired of being
a mouthpiece, the body stuffed sawdust. The head
hard rubber: it would
stretch. Slowly, a glitch

in the intercom grew
to a roar—Dummies and Friends
Together—under the acronym
DAFT. I was daft for sure, followed a different
star, doubted the star in
star lights. *This dummy,* the legend swore, *could*
save a life. Could you?

In the undeclared war
I could save my own, the heart
gone out of it, breath so faint the mirror
refused to cloud. I tried CPR,
turned up the volume, put away the shroud, spoke
at last in my native tongue.

Denby Romany

1

Footloose that year, I borrowed flatware
from the Newman Center—a stainless
steel. I was on loan in Montana, at large
in the world, its crock
swung over my transom. I ducked
going under the lintel, learned to be
cautious and then some: to count
the borrowed dishes—hospital white
like sheets brought from the convent
to this fly-by-night apartment.

Silver and china served me well, as more
and more, I hewed to the earth-tones
I preferred until starter sets of
English stoneware appeared on sale
at the jeweler's. Shy as an uncertain
bride, I touched and hefted
along with the rest, carried two place
settings home to decide on Denby
Romany. I was keeping house
and I must have known.

Sugar bowl, casserole, creamer—piece by
expensive piece, I built from
that early bargain, from earlier bone-white
boredom, the terms of my release.
Romany: a gypsy harmony—sunbrown,
pale gold. Not porcelain with bone-ash,
but clay: dense grain a man
might fancy. I loved the handmade
character, each bowl a free original,
the eye its only mold.

2

Deep Freeze! the kids on the playground
chanted, cryonics in advance. Not
the nickname I always wanted. The evidence
favored staying single. I read
the crude graffiti and locked my sex away,
body-on-ice for the resurrection, horizon
gray, a good man more than

                          hard to find, as
every hour my mother groomed me for a marriage
made in Heaven. All the cloudy morning, the pale
nuns floated by. Never a spot or wrinkle,
the china faces remote as snow-
leopards, painted on high-
shelved plates. I sometimes felt

                          the urge
to cage myself in their credenza. The body
breakable: Temple of the Holy
Ghost. Once breached, it would not mend,
the scarred reminder of engagements
lost. Awkward, ill-fitting body,
always in the way. I would have traded for

willoware and hell-to-pay, except that
catechism was a step
removed from earthquake. Glazed and
fired for disaster, I stalled and held my
tongue. No wonder I can't recall
the child who never was
when I was young.

3

A continent from Montana, far from the china
priest (Dishes had turned me gypsy)
I found in the daunting east another Newman

Center, the human need for touch: held hands
to say the Lord's prayer, my isolation
such that I recalled a story: *Near the end*

the cold and perfect light of Renoir's studio
oppressed him. The remedy was
moving out, a little cloth for cushion

pressed in the palm, to keep the wooden
brush handle from harming tender
skin. I moved along the narrow way and found:

wine in a Romany goblet, the Eucharistic feast
suddenly more than symbol
as this New England priest consecrated

bread and wine. Communion wafers in a Denby
bowl, the match for mine of shredded
wheat. *This is My Body. Take*

and eat. Unbroken days at last assured, I
break my fast at home,
approach the Table of the Lord.

4

Late in her seventh decade, a gypsy in the blood
called awake the woman, and blinking into light

she stood—The Woman of the Burning Palm—sweet
smoke of censers on cathedral air.

The stained glass shed its burden—gold, rose-
red, garnet. Like Renoir

she found richer colors in refusal of the perfect
light. Too late acquainted with the shadow-

self that stalked her, she thought of Dali in
the china shop leading a tethered

bull. Reining in the senses, one at a time by
daylight, she recognized them—

five against the leash when darkness fell. No
wonder everything crashed around her.

5

Heavy as lilac and honeysuckle at mullioned
windows, the passion flower's
red or purple at the gate. Impatiens

massed on all the seeded borders. I count the
revelations of December light.
Vision and afterimage so intense they fuse

stereoscopic in declining sun. This is the
field of late, deliberate mowing,
and this, the aftermath. Both come

to heal the heart split from the head, years
gone. Flowers I have not planted
appear—pure gift—in my garden.

I tend them. They tell me more than
destruction inhabits the volatile air.

6

Today you are in Jerusalem, a good man,
an unbelieving tourist
while far away, I keep as I can the Lord's

Last Supper. There with the Twelve, I ponder
the gift of His Body and yours,
the paradox of living off the page, the image

returned to its maker. In the new translation,
the Psalmist says, *I am like a dish*
that is broken, and the words spill over the

shards of a costly vessel where the potter's
wheel left his mark. I remember
the spikenard Magdalen brought to His Feet,

weeping. Why do you seek out the holy if not
from some need for comfort?

7

And yet, and yet, always that gilt-edged missal,
its verses aimed from the penitent's
core: *Unless you eat My Flesh and drink*

My Blood, you shall not have life. Days overcast,
I have it as never before. Why must the head
deny what the heart knows

for certain? What is this rusty sword (word?)
swung from a thread over the dry-eyed
second of Three Sillies on a basement stair?

Lord, I am not worthy that Thou shouldst enter
under my roof. For a time, like a pillar
of salt, I hung back from Your table,

let others climb over my sandbagged feet, tried
to appear calm as they filed past
on their way to the lacquer

bowl, the glass goblet. The pattern long dis-
continued, I wander the backstreets,
the alleys, looking for Denby Romany in every

antique store. *But only say the word, and my soul*
shall be healed. I say to myself
the word already spoken by a priest friend, now

said again in this poem. *God writes straight*
with crooked lines, says the Portuguese
proverb. Here among shards, I am like a dish

that is broken. I keep repeating the words
so easily said to another.
I give You my clay feet, my crooked lines.

Japanese Carp in the Pond: Maui

These fish are older than I. Every morning I learn
from the koi how to swim in the wind-
ruffled pond: the flow of the tail, the fan of
the fins in water, eyes open
all ways to the shadow-life moving beyond us.

Who knows what goes on under the bridge, the plank
where I plant my feet like an absence, innocent
ginger and cannas swaying on shore
at the scalloped edge of concrete? All day
we ravel and weave in extravagant colors.

The Japanese, years ago, crossbred pure red, black,
and white, renamed the fish *Nishiki goi*
after silks in unique patterns. When the fish
line up like boats to dock against lava rock, I study
genetics. These are the players:

the mean grandfather bullfrog with green tiger eyes
and the paint-streaked fins of a primitive
warrior; the fat white office lecher with walrus
mustache, red-rimmed eyes, and jowls, a hypertensive
scarlet. His dowager mate wears too much blue

eyeshadow. I admire the black-scaled matron's sheer
gown with gold-red underslip, her choker of
rubies; the slim lemon debutante who flips on her side
to arc over oncoming suitors. Mouth-breathers all
by the look of things, we know we are merely feeding

or taking in water. Today we are reading the rock:
plants like incipient palms, small pits
where the fire guttered out with the stone light of
lanterns. We drift into the maze of a green world

mirrored—ti-leaves a fortunate cover—and fade

into obsolescence, our sporting days over, the fight
up the falls shared with salmon, to this
haven of survivors, reflective and ornamental.

The Auger Kaleidoscope*

For Andrew Fetler

In the day residue I remember the dreamlight
comes from beetles, their fat volume—
100-pound paper and four-color plates on a
strip of wall, rack made of nails
carefully spaced and partially
driven. I lift down the book that is not
a mistake and look for the tropic light
concealed in the wings: light I am always lifting
the blind to since the black-and-white pages
fluttered opaque and I watched the skyline flare
with the brilliance of insects. Here,
the scope in my hands, acid-etched
case through less-than

                          symmetrical lenses, I know
my dream is predictive. Light we are moving into
and the light escaping
is hardly random, streams from deflecting mirror
arrangements, the science of optics. See
how the beetle-bright patterns
emerge from their dark confinement, flung
like cathedral windows. Metal
bathed to a brassy sheen in its own corrosive
element outlives the cardboard
children reduced to bottle glass and tricky
reflectors. You wanted the core

                         drawn in fire to
glassy loops and spirals, precise
heat the process requires. I give you unfrozen
motion and more: the smoky quartz of my birthstone,
La Belle Verriere, amethyst,

Chartres and carnelian. You are the man mid-stream,
Christ a stone on his back, a door
screening the gravelight. You turn to the sun
pinned down by a difficult boulder. I am
the daughter come back from the tomb to a dream
of light on the mountain, each rolled-away
stone semi-precious, hand-crafted, hand-cast,
fit for sending a traveler on his way.

*Named for the artist Stephen Auger

About The Author

Madeline DeFrees was born and educated in Oregon. She studied with Karl Shapiro and John Berryman and has taught at the University of Montana, the University of Washington, Seattle University, the University of Victoria (British Columbia), and the University of Massachusetts where she was director of the graduate writing program. For nearly thirty years she was a member of the Sisters of the Holy Names of Jesus and Mary and was known as Sister Mary Gilbert, under which name she published her first collection of poems, *From the Darkroom* (Bobbs-Merrill) in 1964. *Possible Sibyls* is Ms. DeFrees' sixth full-length volume; she is also author of *The Springs of Silence*, a memoir, as well as many reviews and essays. She has retired from teaching and now lives in Seattle where she writes full-time.